The Rainmaker

CHRIS J. MARTINEZ

J. JOSEPH GROUP

The Rainmaker / Chris J. Martinez - 1st ed.
ISBN 978-1-7355869-2-2 (pbk)
ISBN 978-1-7355869-3-9 (eBook)

www.chrisjosephmartinez.com

Table of Contents

Foreword v

Introduction ix

Chapter 1 High-Performance Culture 1

Chapter 2 Review the Tape/Training 11

Chapter 3 Love and Rally Your People 14

Chapter 4 Coach Your People 19

Chapter 5 Why the Desk Manager Most
Often Fails 23

Chapter 6 Service Customer: Up Process 46

Chapter 7 Be a Great Closer 52

Chapter 8 Negotiation: Gross is a State
of Mind 58

Chapter 9   Deal Structures: Lending Criteria . 63

Chapter 10   Switch and Get Rich. 70

Chapter 11   Be a Great Deal Finder. 73

Chapter 12   Huddle Up. 77

Chapter 13   Complacency 80

Chapter 14   Inventory Turn Rate 85

Conclusion 89

About the Author 92

Foreword

In the many decades I've spent in the retail automotive industry, I've been exposed to many General Managers, General Sales Managers, Desk Managers, Sales Managers, Closers, and others with similar titles and responsibilities. I have both met and worked intimately with thousands of managers across the country.

Few actually "get" what it means to be an effective manager, and even fewer have what it takes to reach and maintain the highest levels of success within the industry.

And as the retail automotive industry's leading sales strategist, process strategist, and marketing agent, I can quickly and easily tell when a manager "gets it." Christopher Martinez is one of the few high performers and high achievers in the industry that not only "gets it" but "keeps it," "grows it," "teaches it," and "coaches it."

It has been my pleasure to know and work intimately with Chris over the last decade at two ultra-high-performing dealerships—first in Austin, Texas, and at the time of this writing, in Tulsa Oklahoma.

His practical education, hands-on experience, boots-on-the-ground attitude, work ethic, and proven track record are impressive, as are his openness; genuinely kind heart; and willingness to educate, motivate, and coach his staff (especially other managers) to greatness, both personally and professionally.

The pages you are about to consume contain Christopher's broad stroke as well as his granular strategies, mindsets, and processes, all of which have not only led him to greatness but also led his teams to greatness. His teams have delivered upwards of 1200 vehicles per month--not in just one month but in every month and in a single point store.

So grab your highlighter and open your mind. You now have the keys to the kingdom in your hand, available to refer back to at anytime.

Consume, Learn, Execute, Teach, Coach.

Frank J. Lopes
Author of The 7-Minute Setup
VP of FBDigital

Introduction

I started in my automotive career over eighteen years ago, and I didn't know what a desk manager was until I was seven years in. I started at CarMax, and the best lesson that job taught me revolved around what most desk managers in the business don't do. Through a combination of what I learned there and later learned from great managers on the traditional side of the car business, I arrived at the qualities that make a great (and successful) desk manager.

Most desk managers believe that printing out a four square or saying "No" to a salesperson on a proposed deal is what makes them a strong desk manager. In reality, what makes a great desk manager (or sales manager, the terms are interchangeable) is the ability to be a rainmaker.

A rainmaker, by definition, is a person who generates income for a business. It's a person who brings in new business and wins new accounts, almost by magic. The desk manager is able to be a rainmaker by knowing how to properly put a sale together in order to hold their margin.

You might wonder, *What does "putting the sale together" mean?* In simple terms, it means justifying your price so that the salesperson doesn't think you can—or have to—give up more margin in order to make a deal. Most sales professionals work for the benefit of the dealership—until it means the difference between selling a car and not selling a car, that is. At that point, they start working for the customers, and they often won't hesitate to sell a car at a loss if it means they can get a unit count and a minimum commission.

The desk manager therefore has to be a strategy player. He (or she) has to be on the floor as a floor manager in order to ensure that he can engage with the client and the sales professional simultaneously and early on in the process. He must be able to discern when he needs to intervene as well as how to coach the sales professional when it comes to getting to the next step. This only happens when the desk manager is on his feet. Many desk managers think that just sitting at their desk while waiting for a deal makes them a great manager or leader. Truth: The real magic happens on your feet, on the floor.

If you've ever wanted to become a desk manager—and not just any desk manager but a great one—this book will provide you with the necessary fundamentals. I will highlight key strategies that have helped me over the years in developing not only my own skills but those of countless managers I've been able to work with. If you've wondered what it takes to grow a dealership without all the fancy advertising and gimmicks, I can tell you with certainty that it starts with one car deal at a time, which is why your role as desk manager is critically important.

Above everything else I put forth in this book, remember this quote: "Win without cheating." No car deal is worth your reputation or your career. I promise, if you can't make the deal happen today, work harder to educate yourself and your customer, and you'll likely get the deal tomorrow.

Now that that's out of the way, if you're anything like I was early in my career, you've heard that the desk manager makes the big money. The best desk managers in the industry, in fact, make between $150K and $250K per year, depending on the volume of the dealership.

If you're ready to play at a higher level and start making that next-level income, this book outlines what it takes to be regarded as the best desk manager in your dealership, if not in your group at a national level.

Don't just say that you're ready. Actually, make the commitment to *getting* ready. There's nothing worse than hearing someone say, "Tomorrow I'm going to start my diet," or "Tomorrow I'm going to go to the gym first thing" and then, the next day, you see that person eating a cheeseburger or an entire pizza—and they never went to the gym. If you're the type of person who does this sort of thing, quit reading. Just put the book down and go grab that cheeseburger.

If, however, you're a high-performing individual who wants to reach that next level in your career and make real money, keep reading. What

I'm going to tell you is basic in nature; that's why we call them fundamentals. They're the building blocks you need to tackle each and every day. Not just once or for five days, but every single day for the rest of your career. If you commit to that, I promise that you can make more money and impact more lives than anyone (and everyone) around you.

Looking back, I remember the first time I made this decision for myself. I was about twenty-eight years old, and I remember saying, "I am going to do ten times more than anyone else is doing right now." It was one of the best declarations I ever made. Shortly thereafter, I ran across a book titled *The 10X Rule* by Grant Cardone, which was absolutely amazing. Once I finished reading it, I felt like Grant and I were on the same frequency, and I knew I had made the right decision.

I hope you take these tips, apply them, and see the same level of success (if not more) than I ever did as a desk manager, sales manager, or floor manager. And, always remember, as my good friend Alex Flores says, "Shortcuts equal pay cuts." There are no shortcuts in life or in car sales.

Chapter 1

High-Performance Culture

What kind of leader are you?

Are you holding your people accountable, or are you simply a "grandparent leader"? I was listening to Patrick Bet-David on YouTube just recently. He gave a speech at a Driven event wherein he discussed what a "grandparent leader" is. Nothing against grandparents—what he meant was that most grandparents let their grandkids do whatever they want. I remember that, when I was younger, if my parents told me I couldn't have candy, my grandparents would give me some.

While this is a fun quality to have in *actual* grandparents, don't be a grandparent leader. You must have non-negotiables in your business, and be unwavering in them. You must hire people who fully understand what your non-negotiables are and are willing to stick to them. You almost have to symbolically put a stake in the sand and declare, "These are my non-negotiables, and I will not settle for anything less."

What do non-negotiables look like at our dealerships?

1. Accountability: Team members are required to hit certain minimum benchmarks. They are required to produce at a certain level in order to stay on the team.

2. Treat People with respect: Simply put, our team members are expected to treat people the way they'd want someone to treat their grandparents. This goes for fellow employees as well as customers.

3. Win without cheating: Team members cannot do anything illegal, unethical, or immoral to try to move the company forward.

When building a high-performance team, our team members must live by these principles and be unwavering in them.

While many desk managers also operate as floor managers now and then, if your dealership has a structure wherein you have a dedicated floor manager, keep using that format. However, most stores don't, so in all likelihood you'll have to be on the floor making sure that you can intervene whenever possible. It's like poetry in motion, and the earlier the desk manager can engage with the customer and the sales professional, the wider the margin the manager can hold onto.

In case you're wondering, the same approach applies for stores with a no-haggle philosophy. In this case, the desk manager must jump in early in the process in order to identify where the sales professional is so that he can help push the sale forward. Jumping in early is also a way to help hold the sales professional accountable if he's trying to skip steps. Too often, we have desk managers who want to sit at their desks and just wait until sales opportunities land in their laps. The real rainmakers, on the other hand, are on the floor engaging with customers, proactively securing their margin.

In order to be a great desk manager, you need to start by creating a great culture at your dealership. How do you build a great culture? What type of culture do you already have? In the more than eighteen years I've spent in this industry, I've seen my fair share of the following types of cultures:

Dog-Eat-Dog

I've worked in the dog-eat-dog environment, and although I excelled, I wasn't a fan of the it. It was never a good feeling to go into work and spend my day making sure no one was trying to steal from me. In a commission-based environment, it's easy for people to take advantage of a situation in order to cut you out of a deal. The problem with this environment usually starts at the top, where there is zero accountability taken by the management.

Conservative

A dealership with a conservative view or a corporate structure can be a good environment in which to thrive. However, if left unchecked without proper accountability and benchmarks, the problem you will likely run into can be described as a "slow bleed." It's not sustainable and, at some point, you will go backward. I've found that most underperforming stores were once great, but they lost the accountability piece because they had built such a great relationship with their employees that those employees wouldn't hold them accountable and instead blamed their poor performance on outside economic reasons. I'm not suggesting that you it's not important to have great relationships with your employees. I'm simply saying that, even when you have those great relationships in place, you still need to have the tough conversations with team members when they are under performing. You have to be willing to coach them up or coach them out.

High-Performance (Winning Team)

This is the type of culture I recommend that all organizations cultivate. It combines conservative views with a hard dash of accountability and Key

Performance Indicators (KPIs). KPIs are there to keep teams in line. We all need accountability and discipline in our life, both professionally and personally. For example, if I eat cheeseburgers and fried foods three times a day, I can all but guarantee that at some point I will gain weight or have a heart attack. To better my health and live longer, I need to have a certain amount of discipline in my eating and exercise habits. Sure, I like sitting on the couch and eating pizza and cheeseburgers as much as the next guy, but doing that consistently won't get me to the promised land. When it comes to having a winning team, the KPIs must be there in order to set the standard. If you fall below the benchmarks and never get back up, it shouldn't be a surprise when you are cut from the team.

In order to maintain a winning culture, you must make tough decisions. This doesn't mean that you have to treat your employees badly. It means that if there is poor performance, there are repercussions, in the same way that you may get a speeding ticket if you're caught speeding. I believe in always treating people with respect and making your environment a great one, but a respectful environment doesn't lack accountability. Each of us has to be accountable, or there will ultimately be no business. Here are two examples of how you can respectfully hold your people accountable.

KPIs to Hit Benchmarks

If someone goes ninety days in a row without hitting his objectives, he is moved to another department or terminated.

Tie KPIs to the Pay Plan

In order to qualify for bonuses, an employee has to hit certain metrics. The quickest way to change a behavior is to change the pay plan.

I have found that no matter how hard I tried to lead someone or inspire them to do certain things, the only way I knew for certain that a task would be accomplished was by holding team members accountable. No one likes to be the bad guy, but there is a reason why speeding tickets exist (to return to that analogy). The only way I've been able to successfully change a behavior is by tying results to an employee's pay plan or holding them to certain KPIs in order to stay on the team.

As a father of four, I've had to hold my kids accountable time and time again when it comes to taking their medicine. I've bribed them as well as Googled or YouTubed creative ways to encourage them to take their medicine when they were sick so they could get better. Unfortunately, I've most often had to resort to forcing them to take it. Believe me, there is nothing worse than watching your kid cry as you hold him down to give him medicine. I swear, it hurts me as much as it hurts them. However, in order to get better, sometimes we all need that extra push.

> "A coach isn't your friend. A coach is there to push you beyond what you thought was possible or what you wouldn't do on your own."
>
> —Robert Kiyosaki, *Rich Dad Poor Dad*

In order to win in the game of cars, you must develop a high-performance culture. I've never seen a team be successful without creating and adhering to performance metrics. You also have a passion for this industry as well as for winning. Sometimes, passion is mistaken for aggression. Nick Saban said it best: "Passion always looks like aggression to the unmotivated."

If you're committed to putting together a high-performance team, start with these steps:

1. Make sure that the why or vision is clearly understood.

2. Stress the importance of values—doing things morally, ethically, and legally.

3. Focus on the importance of being customer-centric—without your customers, there is no business.

4. Ensure you have players in the right positions—the right players in the correct positions are the difference makers.

5. Make sure that your team is self-managed.

6. Pay attention to accountability so that goals are achieved.

Chapter 2

Review the Tape/Training

"Training is not what you did, it's what
you do."

—Brad Lea

This statement from Brad Lea is spot-on, and
the same principle applies for role playing
and practicing.

Are you the type of professional who reviews the
tape daily?

What type of preparation are you engaging in?

Are you a student of your craft?

Are you a true professional?

Do you have what it takes to win the game?

If you're a football enthusiast, you may remember the Superbowl when Seattle was trying to beat the Patriots. Instead of using their star running back to score the winning touchdown, they opted for a pass play. Only Malcolm Butler was on his game, and with just twenty seconds remaining and the Seahawks in position to score on the Patriots' one-yard line, Butler intercepted a pass attempt to wide receiver Ricardo Lockette at the goal line, returning possession to the Patriots who maintained their 28–24 lead. Butler later stated that he had guessed correctly that Wilson would throw to Lockette, having read the Seahawks' two-receiver stack formation. "From preparation," he said, "I remembered the formation they were in. I just beat him to the route and made the play."

Are you practicing your craft daily?

Are you pushing yourself to role play daily?

Level up your game. Play at peak performance so that when you are with your customers, it will be as easy as breathing. The process will require little to no thought, and you will come to know exactly which play to call to close each deal.

> "Practice isn't something you do once your good; it's the thing you do that makes you good"

> —Malcolm Gladwell

Chapter 3

Love and Rally Your People

I recently listened to Art Williams, the founder of Primerica, and his message resonated with me. It's critical to build relationships with your people. Art and his team were able to amass an organization of over 225,000 employees, and the level of respect that he has for his people and that they have for him is truly inspiring. From his time as a high school coach, he's loved his people and treated them like his children. He is a true entrepreneurial leader

When you practice the concept of loving and rallying your people in a way you would your children, you have to consider the following two approaches in order to most effectively push them:

Motivate

> "People often say that motivation doesn't last. Well, neither does bathing. That's why we recommend it daily."
>
> —Zig Ziglar

Encourage a Shared Mindset

> "A mentor is someone who sees more talent and ability within you than you see in yourself, and helps bring it out of you."
>
> —Bob Proctor

In a scene from the movie "300", which tells the story of how other countries were going to help the Spartans fight against more than two million soldiers, Daxos says to King Leonidas, "I see I was wrong to expect Sparta's commitment to at least match our own."

King Leonidas responds, "Doesn't it?"

He then points to an Arcadian soldier behind Daxos, asking, "You there, what is your profession?"

The soldier replies, "I am a potter, sir."

King Leonidas then points to another soldier. "And you, Arcadian, what is your profession?"

"I am a sculptor, sir," the soldier replies.

King Leonidas then turns to a third soldier and asks, "You?"

The third soldier responds, "Blacksmith."

King Leonidas then turns back and shouts, "SPARTANS! What is YOUR profession?"

The Spartans respond "HA-OOH! HA-OOH! HA-OOH!"

King Leonidas turns to Daxos and says, "You see, old friend? I brought more soldiers than you did!"

This scene showcases how each of the 300 soldiers shared the same vision. Surround yourself with people who share this mindset. What is your role? And do your people know what their role is?

Your message must be crystal clear. Do your team members want to reach their goals as much as you do? If not, why?

> "I have met cab drivers who are more inspired about how they perform their work than some upper-level managers who seem to have lost any drive for excellence."
>
> —Mark Sanborn, *The Fred Factor*

Are you focused on being the best at whatever you are doing? Stop looking at the person next to you; be the best at what *you* are doing. I've always moved up in roles, not because I was friends with the managers but because I've always taken pride in what I do and wanted to be the best at it—whether it was flipping burgers or selling cars. They say cream rises to the top. Be so good in your position that your managers *beg* you to move up.

Chapter 4

Coach Your People

"A coach isn't your friend. A coach is there to push you beyond what you thought was possible or what you wouldn't do on your own.

—Robert Kiyosaki

To coach is to lead through collaborating, then through directing. A coach is sometimes referred to as a coordinator, facilitator, or mentor, and his job is to encourage and train someone to accomplish a goal or task

If you want to be a successful leader in any industry, coach your people. Love them like you would your children, and lead them into accomplishments they wouldn't have previously thought possible or wouldn't attempt on their own.

The military has a saying: "No man left behind." If someone is wounded, the team gets together and carries him or her back to safety. Military personnel also engage in obstacle courses and other physical challenges where, if a person can't cross the finish line on his own, someone else has to carry that person across it. Sometimes, employees need to be carried across the finish line. We sometimes have to sit right there in front of them and ensure they are making effective contacts. That is why regularly practicing one-on-ones is so important, and you might have to do one every hour with some individuals until they get more comfortable and effective.

I once again think about my kids when it comes to this scenario. I've been teaching them to brush their teeth since Day 1, yet every day I have to push them to do it. I have to hold my four-year-old down and wrestle both him and the toothbrush, and I've been doing it like that every day for four years. I have the same challenge with my six- and eight-year-old. They don't want to brush their teeth, and pretend to be asleep to try to avoid it almost every night. So, it's a constant effort on my part; I know the importance and the value of brushing one's teeth, but it seems as though they won't come to this understanding until later in their lives. Similarly, you'll likely have to hold most of your employees accountable and push them every single day.

A great desk manager has a checklist and does not do all of the work for the salesperson. If the salesperson hands you an incomplete deal, give it back to him and make sure he gets it all correct so that, ultimately, all you have to do is check the deal over and sign off on it. Don't print and do everything for the salesperson or he will never learn or get better. The only way he's going to get better is if you keep pushing him every time to get the documents that he needs and make sure that they are in order.

Further, don't be afraid to be brutally honest when someone is failing. This may hurt both parties in the short term, but it's part of the process of getting better.

Remember, the muscle only grows when it tears. Now, I don't believe in browbeating. However, I do believe in being honest, which sometimes hurts more than browbeating.

> "Don't tell them what they want to hear, tell them what they need to hear."
>
> —Alex Flores

Chapter 5

Why the Desk Manager
Most Often Fails

I've been a desk manager, and I can honestly confess that I failed in the role plenty of times. Each time, I tried to understand what I did wrong so that I didn't do it again!

In order to not repeat history, keep in mind the following parts of the process where a desk manager often drops the next time you're trying to help your sales professionals convert a sale:

He Doesn't Conduct a Proper Interview of the Salesperson

The interview should start with, "Is your customer here?" The reason I ask this question is because of order of importance. If you have more than one deal you're desking, you can put the salesperson who doesn't have a customer in the store on hold.

Next, ask, "Did you test drive your customer?" I am a believer that "the feel of the wheel makes the deal." If your salesperson isn't able to sell the customer on a test drive, take a turn and see where there is a disconnect.

At that point, ask "Did you get the vehicle appraised?" It's important to identify the trade early on.

You can then ask, "Did you get a payoff?" *Make sure you get an accurate payoff*. Remind the salesperson that he's not just *pretending* to make a car deal—he's conducting a real car deal. Answering with an even number is a telltale sign that the salesperson didn't get an accurate payoff.

He Overthinks the Deal or Acts as the Bank

I've seen far too many sales managers want to become the bank and start "dissecting" a customer's credit. Just submit the deal. I've salvaged many deals simply because I took an extra two seconds to submit it. (If you're running a dealership where you still box close, I feel for you. You're probably losing upwards of twenty-five percent of your deals just because of this. And, as scary as it may be, that number is likely higher.)

He's Afraid to Turn the Salesperson

If the dealership is busy, identify a stronger salesperson to take a turn. I understand that the initial salesperson may get mad, but remind him that it's not personal. Half of a deal is better than no deal at all. This is also how you grow your senior sales staff. These individuals will be your future managers, so train them on how to close deals and include them on turns to watch your overall sales grow.

He Doesn't Test Drive Every Customer

A great deal manager understands this saying and pushes their sales professionals to do this for every customer. Remember:

The Feel of the Wheel Makes the Deal!

I've heard this saying again and again over the course of the more than eighteen years I've been in the car business, and recently at our Mercedes-Benz store, I heard the best related story.

A customer walked in looking for her salesperson, and Alex, the manager on duty, introduced herself and asked how she could be of service.

The customer responded, "I would like to buy one of those Wagons that are on a two-year waiting list."

Alex replied, "We actually have a Wagon in stock, and I'll get your sales professional to show you the vehicle."

The salesperson went to get the Wagon, and upon arrival with it, the customer said, "No not that one, the big Wagon."

"Oh, you're talking about the G Wagon!" Alex clarified. "We don't have one in stock, but why don't you take the E Wagon for a spin? It's a very pretty car, and you'll just love it."

The salesperson took the customer on the test drive and showed her the features and the benefits of the vehicle. When they got back from the demo ride, the customer planned to move forward with the purchase of the E Wagon. The feel of the wheel made the deal.

I question whether, if the manager wasn't there, the salesperson would have given the client the option of the E Wagon or instead taken the order on a two-year waiting list vehicle? I've been selling cars for a long time, and my experience tells me that customers do a lot of research, and they *think* they know what they want. However, a true professional will do a guest interview (aka needs analysis) and oftentimes open the customer's eyes to a completely different vehicle. This is what separates a professional from an amateur. The amateur will assume that the customer has spent weeks researching the vehicle of their dreams and only wants that specific vehicle, whereas the true professional will acknowledge the vehicle the customer wants but will also do the guest interview. In in doing so, he will identify the hot buttons and features most important to the customer in order to be able to recommend an alternative option. *Most* importantly, the true professional will always take the customer for a test drive. I've seen the vehicle a customer originally thought he wanted not live up to his expectations once he test drove it more times than I can count.

If you want to win more often than not in the game of cars, always do a guest interview and have options for the customer so that, in the event that the vehicle he wants isn't available or isn't as satisfying as he imagined it would be, you can open his eyes to an amazing alternative. Again, *most* importantly, get him to drive that vehicle. Trust me, he will more than likely love you for it.

He Doesn't Coach (or Understand) How to Conduct a Proper Turn

The proper turn is the point when the salesperson is playing to win, and he understands that he's run out of either time or talent. He's done the job to the best of his ability and is requesting a manager's (or another turn guy's) help.

Although I'm not the type of manager who believes in wholesaling old-age vehicles, I do believe in retailing vehicles no matter how old they are. Depending on the dollar amount of your inventory, each car costs $15-50 per day per unit in carrying costs. So, if you do the math on carrying one vehicle for sixty days on the low end ,it will cost you roughly $900 in carrying costs; on the high end it will cost you $3,000. This is why there is the saying: "Your first lost is your best lost"; every day you hold a vehicle, it costs you money. Know your turn.

The Basic Turn

1. Intro/Rapport Building—become a friend to the customer in two minutes

2. The turn guy should have the write up face down and focus on talking about everything BUT the deal.

3. After a bit of rapport building, re-engage in the deal by asking the following questions

- What do you like about the car you picked?
- Did you drive the car?

   If the customer has a trade, ask him what he likes about his trade, what features he you wishes it had, and whether or not the new car he's buying has the new features he wants?

   *Note: if the turn guy doesn't feel good about any of the responses, **re-demo the car** and/or switch cars.*

4. If you have to re-demo the car, **DO NOT** get the person taking over for on the turn to do this. Do it yourself, or get a senior salesperson if absolutely necessary.

5. Go over the write up and ask for the close.

The turn guy's goal is not to lower the price but rather to hold the gross (the margin). The price should be the *last* point of discussion when it comes to closing the customer.

The "Flying To" Turn

The "flying to" is the point in the turn process when the salesperson introduces the customer to the turn guy because he knows he's run out of time and/or talent.

A scenario like this is admittedly very difficult to turn around, but it's not impossible. Here are the steps to best ensure a successful turn:

1. Engage in a quick ice breaker so you can build rapport on the fly.

2. Ask the customer, "Why aren't you purchasing the car you test drove home?" This type of question accomplishes two goals: It catches the customer off guard with a pattern interruption, and it allows you to determine whether or not the customer has already test driven the vehicle or not.

If the customer hasn't test driven the vehicle, ask him to take it for a five-minute test drive. This also provides a good opportunity to offer a "Borrowed Car Agreement" and let the customer drive it to lunch (at which point they have to return with the car, so you have an opportunity to chat more with them about it).

The Parking Lot Turn

The parking lot turn is an effective strategy when your salesperson has let the customer go and you have to get them to come back inside, or you're outside and can clearly see that the salesperson is about to let the customer go. This type of turn is even harder than the "Flying to," and the step where most desk managers lose gross but here are some effective ways to handle it:

1. Ask the customer, "Why aren't you leaving in the new car you test drove?" Be sure to be smiling when you ask this; the goal is to build rapport *very* quickly.

2. Ask, "If I can help you save an additional $500 or $1,000, can I convince you to stay and do business with us?" This should get the customer's attention and stop real buyers from leaving, even if the salesperson got them upset.

3. Ask, "Did your salesperson get your current vehicle evaluated, because this looks like merchandise we need." By showing interest in their current car, you can oftentimes convince the customer to stay.

4. Get the trade evaluated.

Absence of Lot Awareness

Most desk managers don't have "lot awareness" or strong EQ (emotional intelligence). In short, you must be aware of your surroundings and have enough emotional intelligence to notice when customers look like they are about to leave. In a traditional environment, customers will land in corners of the dealership you're rarely aware of. Deals can slip through the seams of your lot if you're not aware of what's going on in those areas. This also means you need to be looking at *all* of your lot traffic.

I define lot traffic as:

1. Walk-in customers: customers on your lot

2. Internet customers: customers in your digital showroom

3. Phone opportunities: customers calling the dealership

4. Service drive: The service drive provides a *huge* opportunity. These customers are a captive audience, as they are going to be with you for at least an hour while they wait to get their vehicle serviced.

If you're not aware of your surroundings and what the various stages of a car deal look like, you're going to cost yourself a lot of sales. Desk managers need to look at internet opportunities like those customers are actually in their showroom. You don't let a customer come onto the lot without being attended to (I hope), so why would you not ensure that sales professionals are responding to internet queries or phone calls within an hour?

Withholding Information

The worst thing I see happen is, the manager tells the sales professionals not to give the customer all of the information via phone or digital communication. Years ago, this may have been an effective practice, however times have changed. Today, you should be giving the customer as much information as possible to get the customer to come in. Doing so builds trust and keeps everything transparent. Without transparency, the Carvanas, Carmaxes, and Vrooms of the world will continue to take market share from you. The more information the better. It may cost you margin, but you'll gain a customer. Remember, 100% of nothing is nothing. The goal is to sell more cars.

Not Actively Listening to Phone Customers

If you're not actively listening to your customer on the call, you're not doing whatever it takes to identify car deals. Regardless of how many cars you're selling a month as a desk manager, there is downtime throughout the day, and there are certain times when you can jump in and listen to calls that are coming into your dealership. You should be identifying whether a salesperson actually brought the customer in via an appointment or just "broomed" them. Oftentimes, just by listening to the calls, you can identify an opportunity to call the customer back as a manager and turn it into an actual sales opportunity.

Every customer who comes into your dealership through every channel is an opportunity. Look at him as such. The real pros are doing this every day. If a customer walks into your showroom and no one is paying attention or the salesman simply says "Hello" and then lets them leave, that's a missed opportunity.

You need to be actively engaging with phone customers as though they're in the showroom. If the sales professional isn't answering the customer's questions or doing the appropriate needs assessment to help the customer, your dealership is doing that customer a disservice.

If you can apply this type of mentality, your close ratio on phone opportunities should be north of thirty percent. I've personally called back customers who were looking for a specific vehicle and said, "I have similar options in different models that may be even less expensive than what you were looking for. Would you consider these other options if I could save you money?" Only through asking those type of questions was I able to bring those customers into the dealership and sell them a car. You are costing yourself big business if you are not doing this every day.

No Trade Holds

> "Opportunity is missed by most people because it is dressed in overalls and looks like work"
>
> —Thomas Edison

Most desk managers don't get out of their chair to hold the trade because it looks like work. However, by doing so (or, in this case, *not* doing so) they are leaving thousands of dollars on the table.

What are you doing to hold the trade-in? Did you know that CarMax holds $500 on every vehicle? The best in the business engage in early management involvement in order to secure that $500-$1000 (and sometimes a full ten percent) of the value of a vehicle, depending on the price of the vehicle.

How do they do it? They don't rely on the sales professional to do the trade walk-around with the customer. When doing the appraisal, take the customer with you to justify the number. Point out the good things about the vehicle, and touch on all the things that need to be deducted from the trade price. For example: scratches, miles, damage, service history, and check engine lights on the vehicle.

They Don't Engage in Early Management Involvement (EMI)

EMI as a whole is a critical part of the process, and it's why the floor manager is so necessary. Consider the desk manager the quarter back and the floor manager your wide receiver. They are both very important roles that should not be taken lightly.

There are three different types of early management involvement, and each has its own value.

Early Management Introduction

This step gives you an opportunity to say hello to the customer and perhaps do a quick ice breaker to let the customer know you're there to help.

Early Management Involvement

Early management involvement is where the manager gets involved to see where they may be able to get the customer steered in the right direction. Generally, this is where you can do a quick needs assessment to make sure the salesperson is on the right path.

Early Management Intervention

This occurs when the salesperson has clearly taken the customer on the wrong path and the floor manager needs to get a more seasoned sales professional to streamline the process for the customer.

Present the data with a pencil (deal worksheet):

Trade Value	$15,000
Rear Bumper	-$1250
100k mile Service	-$2500
Actual Trade Value	$11,250

Then, communicate with your customer. "Mr./ Mrs. Customer, remember the rear bumper damage you had on the vehicle? We had to put a deduction in there for that, as we will have to fix it in order to list the vehicle for sale. Also, the 100k mile service that is due on the vehicle has to be completed as well. Your actual trade value is $11,250."

If you complete this process with every customer, you will level up your game.

Not Knowing the Metrics

Desk managers need to know how many customers are taken on a test drive each day. They need to know how many customers the dealership has in service. They need to know how many appointments are still scheduled to be coming in each day. They are the dealership's traffic controller, and they knows how to convert deals. This is why we refer to them as rainmakers.

Be obsessed, daily. If you don't have a passion for this business, get out. You have to be willing to go the extra mile every day in order to find the kind of success you're likely dreaming about.

Not clear on the Customer's Objections

Some proven ways to quickly get clear on the customer's objections (so that you can effortlessly counter them) are:

Be seated

Always be seated. If you're standing, invite the customer back to the office and make sure all parties are seated. This will help you get back in control.

Build Trust

As a sales professional, the first thing you must do is build trust. You could simply say, "I want you to feel like you're being treated fairly at all times. So please stop me if you feel like I'm being unfair at any point so we can address it."

Be the Authority

Clarify the deal. Don't give the customer a false sense of hope. You'll be surprised by the power of the word "No." Always reiterate the deal both you and the customer have agreed to. Sometimes, you'll be able to close customers simply by re-explaining the deal. You will find that saying it one more time for the customer to understand is oftentimes all you need.

Question

Ask "how" and "what" questions to draw out any underlining objections. For example: "We unfortunately cannot agree to your terms. What else can we do to help move this deal forward? How can we get to that number knowing what the market values are?"

Mirror your customer

When you don't like an answer the customer has given you, simply repeat the answer the customer provided in an inquisitive way. Watch the you say it; your tone should be low and slow. Pause after you've re-uttered the phrase. You may have to do this several times.

Get the Customer to "That's right!"

This is the *aha* moment! For example, ask, "How did you arrive at this vehicle?" or "What made you pick this vehicle?"

Ask for the Sale

This is where you use your arsenal of closes. For example: "Doesn't it make sense to move forward? All we need is your signature, and then we can start getting the vehicle cleaned and ready for delivery." At this point, hand the customer the pen to sign the write up.

If you want to succeed in this business, you'll have to decide **today** that throughout your entire career, you'll remain committed to doing these things every day. Daily habits turn into excellence.

> "We are what we repeatedly do. Excellence, then, is not an act, but a habit."
>
> —Aristotle

If you want to be a successful desk manager and aren't living by the above motto, you need to start. You need to be having daily one-on-ones and checklists for your staff. I highly recommend that all of my sales professionals and all of my managers maintain a checklist to keep them on task, and remind them to continue to play at a high level. You need to be playing at this high level to generate the bigger payouts you desire.

"In the confrontation between the stream and the rock, the stream wins— not by strength but by perseverance."

—H. Jackson Brown, Jr.

"Start by doing what's necessary; then do what's possible; and suddenly you are doing the impossible."

—Francis of Assisi

"What does brushing your teeth for two minutes achieve? Absolutely nothing unless you do it twice a day, every day. It is the consistency. The accumulation of brushing your teeth day after day that protects them and prevents them from falling out. It would be redundant to measure or find a metric to assess the value of brushing your teeth for two minutes, but rather more reasonable to evaluate this over a longer time frame. For example, if you invest in a new whitening toothpaste, you wouldn't expect this to have an impact after the first brush. Instead, you might review the impact over a weekly or monthly basis."

—Simon Sinek

I just hit you with all of those quotes with the hope that they help you to get the message LOUD and CLEAR.

Chapter 6

Service Customer: Up Process

A great desk manager shows his staff how to back their way into car deals in the service drive. One of my former desk managers showed me how to do this, and it helped me sell thirty cars a month when I was on the floor. You should be able to teach this process to every one of your sales professionals and turn them into real car pros.

We've all had managers who've told us to "work the service drive" and other "up" processes, but have any of them they really shown you how to execute a process that will help you pivot a customer from buying an oil change to buying a car?

Here is a quick six-step process that, when executed correctly, can help your sales professionals sell a minimum of four to five cars per month. You can, of course, help them to sell even more cars using this technique.

I've always been a strong proponent of working different buckets of customers:

1. Walk-ins (5)
2. Phone Ups (5)
3. Internet ups (5)
4. Service Customers (5)
5. Referrals (5)
6. Data Mining (5)
7. Chat (5)

Total: 35 customers

If you work every one of these buckets and you start with two customers in each bucket, you can find success relatively quickly. This is the exact method I used in order to reach thirty plus car sales a month as a sales professional. You can ultimately live off of some buckets entirely in order and get to the bigger numbers of 100+ cars sold per month like Frank Crinite or Ali Reda. They primarily live off referrals, and they are the best at it. They have mastered the art of relationship selling.

Here is the technique I used to help my sales staff work the service customer bucket:

Service Customer | Up Process

Before you have your sales professional greeting all the customers you can cherry pick for them, you, as the desk manager, should be going over all service appointments. Your CRM or data mining solution (I use TheAutoMiner.com) can easily provide you with all the low-hanging customers who already have equity in their vehicle, but don't let this detour you from talking to every customer. I have identified that customers who have to pay over $500 for their service work will consider getting a new vehicle before having to pay for that service work.

Here is the process I've found to be most effective:

1. Check your appearance.
2. Meet and Greet: two-minute rapport building
   - Remember the basics of good communication.
   - Find common ground.
   - Create shared experiences.
   - Be empathic.
   - Mirror and match customer's mannerisms and speech appropriately.

Ask the customer questions about their car.

- What kind of vehicle do you have in service?
- What kind of service is your vehicle in for today?
- How many miles does it have on it?
- Who is your service advisor?

3. Transition into Sales mode

   You could continue by saying, "Since you're waiting anyway, I'm going to go ahead and get with your service advisor to evaluate your vehicle." A common objection to this is: "You don't have to do that; I'm not in the market." Overcome it by reassuring the customer with "Don't worry, it's not a problem at all. I want to make sure you leave here knowing the position you're in. You never know!" At that point, just keep moving. Politely excuse yourself and go see the Service Advisor. Find out exactly where the vehicle is and put it into vAuto or write down all the necessary information to get the vehicle appraised by your manager.

4. Back yourself into a car deal

   • Get the payoff of the customer's current vehicle.

   • Pick out a similar vehicle that is new (or newer than what they have), and have your manager put a deal together.

- Extend their payment term to try to get the payments within range of what they are paying currently. Ideally, you want to present the same payment or, even better, a lower one. In the best-case scenario, the customer has equity in his vehicle, and you can cut him a check while still keeping his payments the same.

5. Get the vehicle and take it as close to the customer as possible.

- Do a walk around on the vehicle.
- Encourage the customer to test drive it.

6. Go over the numbers with the customer.

7. Ask for the sale.

If you follow this process, you will undoubtedly find success in the service drive. I've personally done this thousands of times and been extremely successful at it. If you aren't taking full advantage of the opportunity that comes with each and every one of your daily service drive customers, you are costing the dealership, your sales professionals, and yourself a lot of money.

Chapter 7

Be a Great Closer

A s the desk manager, you have to be one of the strongest closers at the dealership. Better yet, you need to know who on your team is the best closer for each customer's personality type. The idea is to know your strengths in order to make the deal. Put the dealmaker in front of the deal. Be the relationship builder.

Personality types are a huge factor, and they require that you identify strategic ways to close a deal. A true sales professional understands the psychology of the customer, which enables him to better understand how to close a deal. RC Evans first told me about a mechanism that identified four different types of customers. The D.E.C.S

52

system helps you truly understand how to mirror your customers.

D—Dominant/Driver. When you work with this sort of customer, you have to act like them.

E—Ego/Expressive. If you want to close the sale with this person, you need to stroke his ego.

C—Complacent/Amiable. You need to approach these customers in more general, human terms— not through a sterile, business approach.

S—Stable/Analytic. This customer needs to know the numbers, and you need to demonstrate every scenario to him. If you want to close more sales, you need to know and understand these four types of customers.

You must understand the three main learning styles. The VAK tool is helpful in accomplishing this:

Visual learning: For people to better understand what you are saying, you have to write down things as you talk.

Auditory learning: You have to speak up to get your message across.

Kinesthetic learning: This is a combination of both visual and auditory learning whereby customers understand you better when you speak while interacting with physical objects for both audio and visual signals.

Officially closing the sale is one of the most critical steps of the entire car selling process. It's make or break, do or die. Sealing the deal is, in and of itself, an art. Here, too, you need to rely on a combination of skills and techniques. Here are a few basic, time-tested techniques:

Opinion close: Ask the customer's opinion regarding the hurdles to closing the deal.

Assumptive close: Be confident that the customer will make the decision to buy the product.

Now-or-Never close: Set a particular timeline and add scarcity, such as "limited discount offers" to persuade the customer to sign the deal.

Balance-sheet close: Make a list of pros and cons to persuade prospective buyers.

There is a clear and undeniable strategy involved when it comes to closing deals. You need to know when to pull out the worksheet, fill in the equipment list, determine the starting price, fill in the customer details, and add personalized notes. You also need to know when you've potentially called the wrong play, such as attempting to close too soon, trying to close with the wrong person, waiting too long to close, failing to notice the close, and continuing to sell after the close. For more direction on these topics specifically, check out *Driving Sales: What It Takes to Sell 1000+ Cars Per Month.*

You need to know a customer so fluidly that if he raises an objection, you have your counter ready in an instant to overcome it. It's like a boxing match. If someone connects with a right hook, you've got to be able to quickly counter it or you'll get knocked out. *The Closer's Survival Guide* by Grant Cardone is a truly informative and engaging must-read on this subject.

The greatest desk managers know how to connect with people. You almost have to be someone who is great at making friends wherever you go. People buy from people they like, and strong relationships often continue forever. How you treat your customers and how you interact with them personally makes a huge difference. The greats like Ali Reda and Frank Crinite understand this. After the sale, they don't just forget the customer. They call and check in on them periodically. You must have long-term, solid follow-up cadence. There is no alternative or shortcut.

How does this apply to closing the sale specifically? While closing the deal, your focus should not be on the sale itself; it should be on the customer. Don't think simply about how you can sell the car. Instead, consider how many times you can sell a car to this one customer. Think about how many cars you can sell to the people who this customer refers to you. I'm telling you, it's a lot of cars.

You must regularly practice relationship sales techniques in addition to having tact and wit while selling. That level of emotional intelligence leads to the formation of long-term relationships with customers. Were it not for emotional intelligence, salespeople would be extinct in the digital age. People would simply buy everything online.

Sales professional (obviously) still exist, and we're important. One of the tasks we can do far better than a website is build an emotional connection with people—make them laugh, capture their attention, and surprise and amaze them.

Chapter 8

Negotiation:
Gross is a State of Mind

The first time I heard this idea from a previous manager, I thought, *You know, that guy might be on to something!* The value of anything is simply what someone is willing to pay. If you or your sales professional don't believe in the value of what you're selling, you will continue to have low gross. Here is a simple technique to help the "low grosser" on the team hold the margin.

Desk Manager Process

Ask the eight essential questions:

1. Did you test drive the vehicle?
2. Does your customer have a trade?
3. Do you have an exact payoff?
4. Is your customer financing or paying cash?
5. What budget does the customer have?
6. How much are they putting down?
7. How are they going to pay for the taxes?
8. Where's your commitment to buy?

If the salesperson cannot answer any of these questions, send him or her back in to get the questions answered, or turn the salesperson. Call me old school, but your job is to save the customer time *and* make money. If your salesperson isn't asking these questions, he's prolonging the customer's time and costing you a lot of money.

When the salesperson comes back with the answers, start with the Ackerman model of negotiating. Be sure to have an arsenal of closing techniques to help load the sales professional's lips (again, a full outline of the closing techniques I've found to be most successful can be found in *Driving Sales: What It Takes to Sell 1000+ Cars Per Month*). The Ackerman model suggests that customers offer 65%, 85%, 95%, and finally 100% of their final offer. Using the same model while trying to hold margin.

*Note: Before countering any offer, ensure that you have a written commitment to buy 100% of the time.)

Example 1:

- Start your number at 100%. Justify your number and load the salesperson's lips with enough third-party data to close the sale.

- If it doesn't work, drop to 95% of the difference between your and the customer's offer. For example: Your number is $30,000; they are at $25,000. There's a $5,000 difference, so the counter should be $250 off of your original offer. This can often be accomplished by throwing in floor mats, window tint, or other extra features while stressing to the customer that you have a very tight margin.

- If that doesn't work (assuming they have come up on their offer at all), go to 85% of the difference between the two newest offers. For example: The customer goes to $27,000; you're at $29,750. There's a $2,750 difference, so your new counter should be $412.50 off ($29,337.50).

- If that doesn't work (again assuming they came up) and their final number is $28,000 (a difference of $1337.50), your counter and final number should be 65% of the difference, which $468.12. Your final offer would therefore be $28,869.38.

I generally don't recommend going to four pencil negotiations, however for the tougher customers, you'll have to. Ideally, you'll want to have a seasoned sales professional or closer in on the deal sooner than later to flush out any unknown objections. In many cases, you'll find that the real issue isn't about price, and you and the customer are wasting each other's time. Clarifying the deal early on flushes out a lot of the real objections. Early management involvement is key.

As margin compression continues, you'll have to get better at your craft.

> "I fear not the man who practices 10,000 kicks once, but I fear the man who has practiced 1 kick 10,000 times."
>
> —Bruce Lee

Chapter 9

Deal Structures: Lending Criteria

Knowing all lender's criteria is extremely important. It's what separates an average desk manager from a great desk manager. I've made more deals than others over time simply because I knew where to go with the deal. Knowing the type of reserves/flats you could make helped me make deals that an average desk manager wouldn't know.

When structuring a deal, keep in mind that even if you are doing market-based pricing or just marking your vehicles up from cost, it doesn't mean the bank will lend you the full amount. Ask for an intended down payment amount from every customer. The old saying "cash is king" has never been truer.

If you want to hold your margin, it's critical to get the customer to put money down. Most lenders only finance 100-125% of book depending on your market (in Texas and Oklahoma, we use NADA Clean trade). An advance is the total amount the lender will give the consumer as a loan. A 100% advance signifies a clean trade-in value based on the NADA book in Texas and Oklahoma. So, if your advance is higher than that, you'll end up eating the cost or losing a customer if it doesn't fall within your dealer's guidelines.

Be sure to study and be familiar with your lender's guidelines. You need to know which banks use which of the credit bureaus. If a customer has a high score on Equifax, you need to know which banks use that bureau. If you have lenders that will advance 140% of retail book value, you need to know when to send deals to that bank.

For example, if you have a deal that is a 125% advance and the lender's guidelines indicate that their max advance is 110%, cut the deal to 110% and submit it that way to the lender. Once you have the approval, call the bank and negotiate a larger advance. Unless you work for a dealer like CarMax—where they practice "first call best call" and don't allow you to rehash or move your numbers—you want to do this with every credit-challenged customer.

At some point, I suspect that most dealers and banks will get to the same point my former employer reached with a "first call best call" approval approach. It started eleven or twelve years ago, and quickly took the fun out of negotiating with banks for better approvals. However, it did speed up the approval process and made the customer experience more pleasant. It also forced salespeople to get better at selling what they had in stock. The real art is in the relationships you build with your customers, taking care of them so they continue to return to do business with you.

Finally, if you have a deal with an advance of 125%, don't automatically submit it at that if the customer has bad credit. If that is the case, submit the deal based on the lender's guidelines in order to best ensure an approval.

"Show me a strong finance department, I'll show you a strong desk." One of the best car guys I know used to tell me this, and it holds true to this day. Knowing your lender's guidelines will help you find more car deals every day. Knowing which lenders will help with negative equity or heavy advances is key. You goal as a desk manager is to maximize your deals.

Teaching your staff how to plant seeds for backend products is a must. When you pencil car deals, you should be planting seeds on the backend in order to play your key role in helping your finance department make their margin. Work with your finance team on every deal. Like in basketball, set them up for an easy alley-oop.

Time kills deals

I am still dumbfounded when desk managers "pencil" a deal without pulling credit—or worse yet, pull credit and don't know if they can get the customer approved but send the salesperson to go out and close the customer on arbitrary numbers. If you want to sell more cars than you are selling today, just *take the time* to submit every customer before you try to close the customer on the "numbers." Pulling the client's credit is a form of commitment on the client's part, as most customers don't want their credit pulled just for the sake of having their credit pulled. If they agree to have their credit pulled, it typically means they are ready to move forward and make a decision.

Do you truly understand the type of experience your customer is having? Do you know how long it takes your customer to go through the purchase process from start to finish? You need to have a proven roadmap to ensure that your customer isn't waiting any longer than he should.

A timeline that works well for us is:

1. Meet and Greet   1-2 min
2. Fact Finding   3-5 min
3. Vehicle Selection   2-5 min
4. Presentation Demo   5-10 min
5. Trial Close   1-2 min
6. Trade Evaluation/Payoff   5-10 min

7.	Write up	2-3 min
8.	Negotiation/Close	3-8 min
9.	Business Office	30-45 min
10.	Deliver	8-15 min

In the best-case scenario, you can have your customer back on the road in sixty minutes. Worst case, you can get them out in an hour and forty-five minutes (assuming you're efficient). If your customer can't decide right away which car he wants and drives multiple vehicles, your sales process will realistically take a couple of hours. In all cases, there's no point in encouraging your salesperson to stick to a "pencil" deal he isn't sure can get approved.

Keep going until the Bank says No

Even after absorbing all of the previously mentioned information, don't overthink any of your deals. I've seen more finance managers overthink deals, swearing that they knew the call that the bank was going to make, so they failed to submit the deal. Do not overthink the customer's information. Always, *always* submit the deal.

Even when the finance manager believed that there was no way that a customer would be approved, I have had deals approved. In two minutes, I submitted the deal, got it approved, and got the customer further down the road toward his purchase. I wasn't able to do this because I was a better manager; I was able to do this because I actually submitted the deal.

Note: You will receive more approvals by submitting the deal in line with a bank's lending criteria. Don't be so naïve as to think that submitting a deal at 150% of book is what you want, and if the bank wants the deal, they will have to approve it that way. On the contrary, you have to submit in with their lending criteria or they'll return an automatic decline.

Chapter 10

Switch and Get Rich

M ost desk managers get comfortable when they start making $12k a month. The only reason they don't make more is that they don't do all the little things to maximize their car deals or sell more cars.

As a desk manager, you should be identifying the type of vehicle the sales professional has landed on for a customer. If a customer is too payment unrealistic, you need to re-interview the customer. This will help you hold onto the margin and keep your gross average high.

I've seen it time and time again—a sales manager takes the sales professional's word for it, and it costs them thousands of dollars in dealer margin simply because they did not take the time to re-interview the customer. The customer would've been happy to get the payment they wanted on a less expensive vehicle versus the platinum vehicle the sales professional landed on for them. It's okay to re-interview the customer just to clarify you're on the right vehicle even before you drop numbers. If you find that you're on the wrong vehicle, land the customer on the right one and re-demo them. This will save you a lot of heartache and a lot of time. In fact, it will have not only your time but also the customer's time, and it will help you get closer to a car deal.

Also, if you don't submit your deals to the bank from the desk and are relying only on the finance manager to submit them, remember that you don't want to look at declines as the final deal. I had a sales manager submit a deal on a new car, and he told me all of the approvals came back with $4000 in bank fees due to the customer's challenged credit. I simply looked at the vehicle, saw the advance, restructured the deal to keep it in line with the lender's guidelines, and switched cars to a preowned vehicle. It was less expensive and got the deal done with only a $600 fee.

When filling out a credit application, be sure to get with your lenders to clarify how they want you to structure a customer's rent or mortgage payments. In my experience, they want the payment split if the customer is a husband and wife. For example, if the mortgage payment is $2000, don't put $2000 for the husband and $2000 for the wife. Put $1000 for each.

There is an internal score when it comes to how much information a credit application has. If the customer has lived at their residence for one year or less, you'll need to get their previous address. The more information you put on the credit application, the better your chances of raising that internal score. The goal is to have a clearly defined credit application so that the bank can automatically approve your deal. More approvals increase your chances of selling more cars.

Chapter 11

Be a Great Deal Finder

"Put the deal maker in front of the deal."

—Jim DiMeo

My mentor and business partner, Jim DiMeo, is the car guy amongst car guys. One of the messages he consistently drove home in his meetings was, "Put the deal maker in front of the deal."

In the car business, the floor manager must get involved in the deal as soon as possible to help direct the process in order to help close the deal. It's critical that the desk manager acts as the floor manager if the dealership doesn't have someone who occupies that role full-time. Any floor manager who thinks that his primary function is closing deals or doing one-on-one coaching is wrong.

The deal maker is the "restaurant manager"—there to help guide the sales process toward closed car deals. I can't tell you how often I've seen early management involvement help push the process to the next step. We have a saying we use with our sales staff: "If you're not with a customer, then you're prospecting." Similarly, if you are a sales manager, BDC manager, finance manager, or floor manager, "If you're not with a deal, then you're finding a deal." This is the mindset of the best deal makers.

6 EFFECTIVE WAYS TO FIND CAR DEALS

Go through all missed trade evaluations

The best of the best buy or trade-in at 65%, and the average dealer buys at 30%. Having your managers re-look at a trade or call the customer and offer more incentive helps turn a missed opportunity into a deal.

Go through logged walk-in clients

The very best say they close at 40% when, in reality, if you do a better job of logging all your clients, you'll find that you're closer to 10%.

Appointments

Dealers have, on average, a 50% show ratio and a 50% close ratio on shown appointments. Go through the 75% of the customers who didn't come in or buy.

Internet leads

I've seen dealers close at 20-25% on internet leads, and I've seen them close at 9-10%. There are deals here. Go through them.

Phone Calls

If you are only listening to your incoming calls daily, you're missing deals. Sixty percent of the time, the inbound call is being logged.

Revive "The Dead Deal"

These are the deals finance managers (and even desk managers) have attempted to make but weren't successful. Every now and then a fresh set of eyes can find a different way and defibrillate the car deal. Be sure to engage with your customer on the showroom floor as well as the lot. There is nothing more important than the customer who is in the building. All hands should be on deck when a customer is on the premises in order to help guide him into being the happy owner of a new or used vehicle.

Use these simple reminders to work together to find car deals, and you'll be on your way to get those extra two to three deals a day.

Chapter 12

Huddle Up

Do you have daily meetings? Are you having more meetings than your team can handle? Are you having meetings just to have meetings? If you've run into these types of questions, this section is for you.

Ideally, if you want to have productive meetings or "huddles," as we call them, you should be having them every couple of hours. Ideally you want these meetings to be effective and to regroup your team so that they can better focus on why they're there. Five to ten-minute minute meetings work perfectly. If meetings are any than that, you'll lose people's attention. These quick huddles a a great way to keep your team in the game and give them a level of accountability if they aren't on task. You'll be able to clearly see who's working and who isn't.

TIPS TO A SUCCESSFUL HUDDLE

Roll Call

- Identify who is staying on task.
- Identify wins.
- Identify how many customers each sales-person has had and what he has done with those customers. Ask about contact with customers in the areas of Internet, phone, walk-in, and service.

Identify Outreach

- Identify how many outbound calls has your team made, including daily work-plan/prospecting calls, texts, and emails. I like to see who is being productive. There is nothing worse than seeing someone who works on commission in the dealership and is doing nothing.

Note: if you want a high-performance team, doing nothing should not be acceptable. That person shouldn't be working for you.

- How many of those outreach attempts have converted to an appointment?
- How many appointments have shown up versus no-shows? How many rescheduled?

Staying on top of your business is crucial to keeping your team focused and making money. If you do not inspect what you expect, it won't get done. Keeping your finger on the pulse is crucial to your success.

Chapter 13

Complacency

When one is complacent, he or she shows smug or uncritical satisfaction with himself or his achievements. We've all seen the "five-year manager" or the manager who has done a great job, but as is the case with an effective workout routine, you have to change it up now and then in order not to plateau.

Inspecting what you expect is key to not going backwards or hitting a plateau (and staying there). I always look at the following year-over-year comparisons when it comes to total customers versus close ratios in order not to fall prey to this pitfall. It's part of knowing your numbers.

Market Reports

How big is the pie, and is someone taking your market share? I tend to believe that everyone's fighting for your customers, so you need to work just as hard every day. There are a lot of resources to determine how many vehicles are selling in your market. Don't just compare yourself with the franchise you're a part of. How do you stack up against all the dealers in your market?

Web Traffic

How are your conversions from website visits and lead forms?

Phone call engagement

Don't just look at the calls your sales staff have deemed sales calls. Look at *all* the calls. What do your calls to conversions number look like? I haven't seen a store yet, no matter how good they are, that cannot do better on the phones.

Lead Response time

Are you inspecting this, or are your internet managers too busy trying to switch customers out of "internet lead" to another source to make their response time look better? The first sales professional who gets in contact with the customer usually wins the customer. Remember, the customer isn't just filling out a lead with your dealer. They are shopping from every other dealer as well.

Lead handling

Do you have a performing sales funnel? Is there real engagement with the emails you're sending out? Is your sales staff utilizing all forms of contact (i.e., phone, video messages, and email Messenger Facebook)?

Walk-in engagements

Generally, most everyone will tell you that we "dealers" as an industry only log about half of the customers who walk into our showrooms. My buddy has a software that can tell you how many customers actually walked in so that you can compare how many were actually logged. (Of course, your walk-in customers must have a cell phone on them for it to work.)

Service Retention

Are you building your infrastructure to be able to take in more business, or are you relying on walk-in traffic alone?

Sales Retention

Do you have a long-term strategy in place to continue to bring your customers in the door, or are you just relying on the traditional methods?

Merchandising

Merchandising is something most desk managers forget. They don't look at the way their lot looks. This is crucial; you must ensure that you have a presentable showroom not just inside but outside as well. Know where your inventory is. If you have vehicles that were traded in weeks ago and are still sitting in the back, you have a problem. More importantly, if you're not taking your staff for a lot walk every day to identify aged units and fresh trades, you're missing a huge opportunity. This simple practice will help you specifically when it comes to aged inventory as well as determining why some of your fresh trades aren't through service yet.

If your numbers are down in any of these categories, get with your marketing and sales team to shore up these areas.

Chapter 14

Inventory Turn Rate

Every new/used car manager should know their inventory turn rate.

The trend is your friend. As a new or used car manager, you have to understand where your inventory is at all times. As a new car Manager, there is no difference. Know your numbers.

When it comes to inventory, "the Turn" is a topic I've found every manager talking about, but none of them could ever really tell me what it truly means or how to grow your inventory (what metrics to use). As my mentor always said, "Numbers don't lie, people do."

After a bit of research, I was able to identify three metrics when it came to my inventory in both new and used cars. These metrics allowed me to know exactly when to buy more cars and when to slow down. We have a unique situation at our dealership: limited space. Although we've sold 1,000+ cars per month several times, we average 920 cars each month, and unless we buy more land or can figure out a way to turn them faster, we will continue to hover around these numbers. With the lack of space, we have to be very efficient.

Knowing these numbers can help you increase your sales. I don't recommend buying 1,000 cars in one month, but rather, identifying your turn and growing into greater purchasing practices.

Here are the three metrics you need to know:

Sales to Inventory ratio

By knowing this number, you can actually increase your inventory accordingly in order to increase sales volume. You have to do three things in order to ensure that you're not just buying cars to buy cars.

- Monitor the numbers weekly.
- Buy cars at auction or off the street if you're not taking in enough on trade.
- Make sure your days in inventory are consistent and have no more than a five-day variance. The higher the number, the higher the risk that aged inventory comes into play. At that point, you'll have to slow down your buying (or make it easy and just get rid of your aged-car problem).

Retail Turn

This metric is important to understand for two reasons:

1. You don't want to have too much inventory if your team has already set a target to hit.
2. If you have too much inventory, you can have an aged-inventory issue and be underwater real fast. No one wants this problem.

Wholesale Turn

This metric is important in terms of whether your recon team is being consistent. It allows you to monitor your trade volume.

Really knowing your numbers and not just "having a feeling" will get you to the next level. Knowing when to stop buying cars (or when it's too late and your month's almost over to start buying cars) is no longer an issue when you know your numbers.

Remember to really audit your inventory. Don't rely solely on the manufacturer, your buyer, or your inventory manager.

Conclusion

I have had the privilege to work with some of the best in the industry. I push the people around me—not because I believe I'm better but because I know they can be better. There is nothing worse in my mind than wasted talent. One of the sayings that drives me is by Erma Bombeck: "When I stand before God at the end of my life, I would hope that I would not have a single bit of talent left, and could say, 'I used everything you gave me.'" This drives me every day. We only get one life, and if you're going to spend some of it away from your family, make that time it worth it. Maximize your day, and help your people grow.

At a training I conducted fifteen years ago we did an exercise that made us think logically. The premise of the exercise was, if you were a new manager and you went into an underperforming store, what would you do in the next thirty days to turn it around? I ask myself this same question every month, no matter how many vehicles my stores are selling. No matter how successful we become, I do this.

In my mind, I am always wondering, "What is going to put me out of business" and "How am I going to turn this around?" They say success is a lousy teacher because when doing better than they ever have, most people don't wonder how they can do better. I always look back on the month and ask, "Could we have found one more car a day?" The answer is always yes.

If you too can get into this practice every month, I promise you will never have any surprises and you will always be able to grow your dealership to the next level. Once you get in the habit of leveling up, it doesn't get easier; you simply get stronger. I promise, if you keep getting more and more uncomfortable, you will get stronger and be better for it. If you can commit to doing this for the rest of your career, you will have a long and fruitful one. You will be among the best of the best, and the people around you will be a reflection of your hard work. This will help you live a larger life for you, your family, and everyone who surrounds you.

About the Author

When Chris Martinez entered the car sales industry in 2003, he had no definitive sense of direction. Even with successful mentors, he had to make his own way in an increasingly competitive and difficult environment. Chris set out to become the number one salesperson at his dealership and went on to write three bestselling books:

The Unfair Advantage: Digital Marketing Principles That Will Explode the Growth of an Auto Dealership

Driving Sales: What It Takes to Sell 1,000 Cars A Month

The Drive to 30: Your Ultimate Guide to Selling More Cars Than Ever